Appetizing Pizza Recipes for your Grill

A New Grilling Skill, Start Cooking Pizza on the Grill

BY

MOLLY MILLS

Copyright © 2019 by Molly Mills

License Notes

No part of this book may be copied, replicated, distributed, sold or shared without the express and written consent of the Author.

The ideas expressed in the book are for entertainment purposes. The Reader assumes all risk when following any guidelines and the Author accepts no responsibility if damages occur due to actions taken by the Reader.

An Amazing Offer for Buying My Book!

Thank you very much for purchasing my books! As a token of my appreciation, I would like to extend an amazing offer to you! When you have subscribed with your e-mail address, you will have the opportunity to get free and discounted e-books that will show up in your inbox daily. You will also receive reminders before an offer expires so you never miss out. With just little effort on your part, you will have access to the newest and most informative books at your fingertips. This is all part of the VIP treatment when you subscribe below.

SIGN ME UP: *https://molly.gr8.com*

Table of Contents

Delicious Pizza Recipes 6

Recipe 1: Classic White Pizza 7

Recipe 2: Easy Four Cheese Pizza 9

Recipe 3: Canadian Style Bacon Pizza 12

Recipe 4: Simple Veggie Pizza 14

Recipe 5: Delicious Smoked Salmon Pizza 17

Recipe 6: Delicious Shrimp and Artichoke Alfredo Pizza 19

Recipe 7: Gametime Beer Pizza 22

Recipe 8: Healthy Fruit Pizza 25

Recipe 9: Healthy Green Veggie Pizza 28

Recipe 10: Classic New York Style Pizza 31

Recipe 11: Classic Pizza al Forno 34

Recipe 12: Classic Gold and White Pizza 36

Recipe 13: Lazy Cheeseburger and Sausage Pizza 38

Recipe 14: Personal Pan Mushroom Pizza 40

Recipe 15: Garlic Style Chicken Pizza 42

Recipe 16: Tasty Tomato and Spinach Pizza 45

Recipe 17: Spaghetti Style Pizza 48

Recipe 18: Healthy Eggplant Style Pizza 50

Recipe 19: Chicago Style Pizza 52

Recipe 20: Vidalia Style Ranch Pizza 55

Recipe 21: Simple Artichoke and Garlic Pizza 58

Recipe 22: Crab Smothered Pizza 60

Recipe 23: Mexican Style Pizza 63

Recipe 24: Avocado and Asiago Pizza 66

Recipe 25: Greek Style Pizza 68

About the Author 70

Don't Miss Out! 72

Delicious Pizza Recipes

AAAAAAAAAAAAAAAAAAAAAAAAAAAAAAAAAAAAAAAAAAAAAA

Recipe 1: Classic White Pizza

This is another one of my personal favorite pizza recipes and once you have a taste of it yourself, it will become your favorite as well.

Yield: 1 Pizza

Cooking Time: 25 Minutes

List of Ingredients:

- 2 Tablespoons of Butter, Fully Melted
- 1 tablespoon of Olive Oil, Extra Virgin Variety
- 3 Tablespoons of Garlic, Minced
- 2 Tablespoons of Tomato Pesto, Sun Dried Variety
- 1 teaspoon of Basil, Dried
- 1 teaspoon of Oregano, Dried
- 1 tablespoon of Parmesan Cheese, Finely Grated
- 1 Cup of Alfredo Sauce, Your Favorite Kind
- 2 Cups of Chicken Breasts, Fully Cooked and Finely Diced
- 1 Pizza Crust, Prebaked Variety
- 1 Tomato, Medium in Size and Finely Sliced
- 1 Pack of Feta Cheese, Finely Crumbled

Instructions:

1. The first thing that you will want to do is preheat your oven to 375 degrees.

2. While your oven is heating up use a small sized bowl and mix together your first 8 ingredients together until thoroughly combined.

3. Arrange your cooked chicken on top of your prebaked pizza crust and pour your alfredo mixture over the top generously.

4. Top off with your tomato and crumbled feta cheese.

5. Place into your oven to bake for the next 10 to 15 minutes or until your crust is light brown in color and your toppings are lightly toasted.

6. Remove and serve whenever you are ready.

Recipe 2: Easy Four Cheese Pizza

If you are not a huge fan of pizzas smothered with various toppings, then this is the perfect pizza dish for you. This pizza is smothered in 4 different types of cheese that will leave you wanting more.

Yield: 1 Pizza

Cooking Time: 35 Minutes

List of Ingredients:

- 1 Premade Pizza Dough
- 1 Red Pepper, Sweet, Large in Size and Finely Chopped
- 1 Green Pepper, Large in Size and Finely Chopped
- 1 Cup of Mozzarella, Finely Shredded
- ¾ Cup of Swiss Cheese, Finely Shredded
- ½ Cup of Parmesan Cheese, Finely Grated
- ½ Cup of Feta Cheese, Crumbled
- 2 Tablespoons of Parsley, Fresh and Minced
- 1 tablespoon of Basil, Fresh and Minced
- 3 Tomatoes, Plum Variety and Thinly Sliced
- 1 tablespoon of Olive Oil, Extra Virgin Variety
- 2 Cloves of Garlic, Minced

AAAAAAAAAAAAAAAAAAAAAAAAAAAAAAAAAAAAAAAAAAAAAA

Instructions:

1. On a lightly floured surface, roll out your pizza dough into a medium sized circle. Transfer your dough to a pizza pan and build up the edges slightly. Prick over with a fork.

2. Place into your oven to bake at 400 degrees for the next 8 to 10 minutes or until light brown in color. After this time remove from oven.

3. Then reduce the heat of your oven to 375 degrees.

4. Top your pizza dough with your remaining ingredients.

5. Place your pizza back into your oven to bake for the next 15 to 20 minutes or until your cheese is completely melted.

6. Remove from oven and allow to stand for 5 minutes before serving.

Recipe 3: Canadian Style Bacon Pizza

Bacon itself is absolutely delicious, but a pizza made with Canadian bacon is especially delicious. This pizza is easy to make and is guaranteed to become a fan favorite in your household.

Yield: 1 Pizza

Cooking Time: 15 Minutes

List of Ingredients:

- 1 Loaf of Bread, French Variety
- ¼ Cup of Butter, Completed Melted
- 2 Cups of Marinara Sauce, Your Favorite Kind
- 16 Slices of Bacon, Canadian Style
- 1 Can of Pineapple, Unsweetened Variety and Drained
- ½ Cup of Green Peppers, Finely Chopped
- ¼ Cup of Onions, Green in Color and Finely Chopped
- 2 Cups of Mozzarella, Finely Shredded

AAAAAAAAAAAAAAAAAAAAAAAAAAAAAAAAAAAAAAAAAAAAAAAAAA

Instructions:

1. The first thing that you will want to do is cut your bread in half first lengthwise and then again widthwise.

2. Next place your bread with the cut side down facing up onto a baking sheet lined with some aluminum foil.

3. Then brush your bread with some butter.

4. Place into your oven to bake at 450 degrees for the next 5 minutes or until light brown in color.

5. After this time pour your marinara sauce over the top of your bread and top off with your Canadian style bacon and next 4 ingredients.

6. Place back into your oven to bake for the next 8 to 10 minutes or until your cheese has fully melted.

7. Remove from oven and serve right away.

Recipe 4: Simple Veggie Pizza

If you are looking to enjoy a healthier slice of pizza, then this is the type of pizza I know you are going to want to make. Packed full of healthy and delicious veggies, you will never feel guilty about having a slice of this pizza.

Yield: 1 Pizza

Cooking Time: 15 Minutes

List of Ingredients:

- 2 Packs of Crescent Rolls, Ready Made and Refrigerated
- 1 Cup of Sour Cream
- 1 Pack of Cream Cheese, Soft
- 1 tablespoon of Dill Weed, Dried
- ¼ teaspoons of Salt, Garlic Variety
- 1 Pack of Ranch Dressing, Dry Mix
- 1 Onion, Small in Size and Finely Chopped
- 1 Stalk of Celery, Sliced Thinly
- ½ Cup of Radishes, Fresh and Cut into Halves
- 1 Bell Pepper, Red in Color and Finely Chopped
- 1 ½ Cups of Broccoli, Fresh and Finely Chopped
- 1 Carrot, Fresh, Peeled and Finely Grated

AAAAAAAAAAAAAAAAAAAAAAAAAAAAAAAAAAAAAAAAAAAAAAAA

Instructions:

1. The first thing that you want to do is preheat your oven to 350 degrees. While your oven is heating up grease a jellyroll style pan with a generous amount of cooking spray.

2. Next add your crescent rolls into your greased pan and allow to rest for 5 minutes. Piece your dough with a fork all over the surface.

3. Place into your oven to bake for the next 10 minutes. After this time remove and allow to cool.

4. Use a medium sized bowl and mix your next 5 ingredients together until thoroughly combined. Spread this freshly made mixture on top of your cooled dough.

5. Then arrange your remaining ingredients on top of your creamy mixture.

6. Cut into small squares and serve right away.

Recipe 5: Delicious Smoked Salmon Pizza

This is a great tasting pizza recipe that your average seafood lover is going to want to enjoy over and over again. Easy to make and incredibly filling, you just can't go wrong when making this pizza.

Yield: 6 Small Pizzas

Cooking Time: 20 Minutes

List of Ingredients:

- 6 Pita Breads
- ¼ Cup of Pizza Sauce, Your Favorite Kind
- ¼ pound of Salmon, Smoked and Finely Chopped
- 1 Red Onion, Small in Size and Cut into Halves
- 1 Cup of Mozzarella, Finely Shredded
- ¼ teaspoons of Oregano, Dried

AAAAAAAAAAAAAAAAAAAAAAAAAAAAAAAAAAAAAAAAAAAA

Instructions:

1. First place your pita bread onto an ungreased baking sheet.

2. Top your pita breads with your favorite pizza sauce and your remaining ingredients.

3. Place into your oven to bake at 425 degrees for the next 10 minutes or until your cheese is fully melted.

4. Remove and serve whenever you are ready.

Recipe 6: Delicious Shrimp and Artichoke Alfredo Pizza

Artichoke Alfredo Pizza is naturally a delicious type of pizza that I know you are going to want to make over and over again. This particular recipe is easy to make and will leave you wanting to make more.

Yield: 1 Pizza

Cooking Time: 20 Minutes

List of Ingredients:

- 1 teaspoon of Olive Oil, Extra Virgin Variety
- ½ Pound of Shrimp, Large in Size, Peeled, Deveined and Uncooked
- 1/8 teaspoons of Red Pepper Flakes, Crushed
- 1 Pizza Crust, Prebaked
- ¾ Cup of Alfredo Sauce, Premade
- 1 Jar of Artichoke Hearts, Fully Marinated and Drained
- 2 Tablespoons of Tomatoes, Sun Dried Variety, Drained and Finely Chopped
- 1/3 Cup of Cheese, Mozzarella Variety and Finely Shredded

AAAAAAAAAAAAAAAAAAAAAAAAAAAAAAAAAAAAAAAAAAAAAAA

Instructions:

1. The first thing that you will want to do is preheat your oven to 450 degrees.

2. While your oven is heating up heat up your olive oil in a medium sized skillet placed over medium to high heat. Once the oil is hot enough add in your next 2 ingredients and cook for at least 2 minutes or until your shrimp turn pink in color.

3. Next arrange your prebaked pizza crust onto an ungreased baking sheet.

4. Top your crust with your remaining ingredients plus your cooked shrimp.

5. Place into your oven to bake for the next 12 to 15 minutes or until your cheese is fully melted.

Recipe 7: Gametime Beer Pizza

Just as the name implies this is the perfect pizza recipe to make during the football season or baseball season. It is incredibly delicious and will certainly leave you wanting more.

Yield: 2 Pizzas

Cooking Time: 30 Minutes

List of Ingredients:

- 1 tablespoon of Olive Oil, Extra Virgin Variety
- ½ Pound of Sausage, Pepperoni Variety and Finely Diced
- 1 Pound of Bacon, Finely Diced
- 1 Can of Mushrooms, Drained and Finely Sliced
- 1 Onion, Finely Chopped
- 1 Green Bell Pepper, Finely Chopped
- 1 Can of Tomato Sauce, Your Favorite Kind
- 1 Cup of Beer, Light and Your Favorite Kind
- 1 Clove of Garlic, Minced
- 1 teaspoon of Oregano, Dried
- ½ teaspoons of Thyme, Dried
- ½ teaspoons of Salt, For Taste
- 2 Pizza Crusts, Premade and Unbaked
- 1 Pack of Mozzarella, Finely Shredded

AAAAAAAAAAAAAAAAAAAAAAAAAAAAAAAAAAAAAAAAAAAAAAAA

Instructions:

1. The first thing that you will want to do is preheat your oven to 450 degrees.

2. Then heat up your olive oil in a large sized skillet placed over medium heat. Once the oil is hot enough sauté both your pepperoni and bacon together and cook until brown in color.

3. Next mix in your next 3 ingredients. Continue to cook for the next 5 minutes or until tender to the touch. Remove from heat and set aside.

4. Mix in your remaining ingredients except for your pizza crusts and cheese until thoroughly combined.

5. Spread your premade pizza crusts over 2 pizza pans and top with your mixed toppings.

6. Spread your mozzarella evenly over the top.

7. Place into your oven to bake for the next 20 to 25 minutes or until your cheese is fully melted and your crust is golden brown in color.

8. Remove and serve whenever you are ready. Enjoy.

Recipe 8: Healthy Fruit Pizza

While I know adding fruit to a pizza may not seem like the tastiest thing in the world to do, your views will change once you get a taste of this pizza for yourself.

Yield: 1 Pizza

Cooking Time: 20 Minutes

List of Ingredients:

- 2 Cups of Flour, All Purpose Variety
- ½ Cup of Sugar, Confectioner's Variety
- 1 Cup of Butter, Cold
- 1 Pack of Cream Cheese, Soft
- 1/3 Cup of Sugar, White
- 1 teaspoon of Vanilla
- 2 Cups of Strawberries, Fresh and Cut into Halves
- 1 Can of Oranges, Mandarin Variety and Drained
- 1 Cup of Blueberries, Fresh

Ingredients for Your Glaze:

- ½ Cup of Sugar, White
- 2 Tablespoons of Cornstarch
- 1 Cup of Pineapple Juice, Fresh
- 1 teaspoon of Lemon Juice, Fresh

AAAAAAAAAAAAAAAAAAAAAAAAAAAAAAAAAAAAAAAAAAAAAAAA

Instructions:

1. Use a large sized bowl and mix together your flour and confectioner's sugar together until evenly mixed.

2. Cut in your butter and mix until your mixture is crumbly.

3. Press this mixture into an ungreased pizza pan and place into your oven to bake at 350 degrees for the next 10 to 15 minutes or until light brown in color.

4. While your crust is baking use a small sized bowl and beat together your next 3 ingredients with an electric mixer until smooth in consistency. Spread this mixture over your baked crust.

5. Then arrange your remaining ingredients except for your glaze ingredients on top of your spread.

6. Next prepare your glaze. To do this mix all of your glaze ingredients together in a small sized bowl until thoroughly combined and smooth in consistency.

7. Serve your glaze alongside the pizza as a dipping sauce and serve whenever you are ready.

Recipe 9: Healthy Green Veggie Pizza

If you are looking for a healthier pizza recipe to enjoy, this is the perfect pizza dish for you. It is not only incredibly healthy to enjoy, but it tastes amazing as well.

Yield: 1 Pizza

Cooking Time: 35 Minutes

List of Ingredients:

- 1 Mushroom, Portobello Variety and Finely Sliced
- 1 Zucchini, Small in Size and Finely Sliced
- ¼ Pound of Butternut Squash, Peeled, Seeded and Finely Sliced
- 1 Cup of Broccoli, Cut into Florets
- ¼ Cup of Onion, Red in Color and Finely Sliced
- 1 tablespoon of Olive Oil, Extra Virgin Variety
- 1 Premade Pizza Crust
- ¼ Cup of Pesto, Fresh
- ¼ Cup of Gorgonzola Cheese, Finely Crumbled
- ¼ Cup of Fontina Cheese, Cut into Small Cubes

Instructions:

1. The first thing that you will want to do is preheat an outdoor grill to high heat.

2. While your grill is heating up place your first 5 ingredients in a large sized grill pan and toss with your olive oil.

3. Place your pan onto your grill to bake for the next 5 minutes or until tender to the touch. Remove from your grill and set aside.

4. Next roll out your pizza dough onto a lightly floured surface and make it into a medium sized circle. Brush the top of your dough with some olive oil.

5. Place into your grill to bake until brown in color on all sides.

6. Remove your crust from the grill and spread with your pesto.

7. Top off your pizza with your grilled veggies and two types of cheese.

8. Place back into your grill and cook until your cheese completely melted. Remove from grill and serve whenever you are ready.

Recipe 10: Classic New York Style Pizza

If you are a huge fan of New York Style Pizza like I am, then you need to try making this pizza dish for yourself. Once you get a taste of one slice of this pizza, you will never want to make any other type of pizza again.

Yield: 1 Pizza

Cooking Time: 1 Hour and 25 Minutes

Ingredients for Your Dough:

- 1 teaspoon of Yeast, Active and Dry
- 2/3 Cup of Water, Warm
- 2 Cups of Flour, All Purpose Variety
- 1 teaspoon of Salt, For Taste
- 2 Tablespoons of Olive Oil, Extra Virgin Variety

Ingredients for Your Toppings:

- 1 Can of Tomato Sauce, Your Favorite Kind
- 1 Pound of Mozzarella, Finely Shredded
- ½ Cup of Romano Cheese, Finely Shredded
- ¼ Cup of Basil, Fresh and Roughly Chopped
- 1 tablespoon of Oregano, Dried
- 1 teaspoon of Red Pepper Flakes, For Taste
- 2 Tablespoons of Olive Oil, Extra Virgin Variety

Instructions:

1. First sprinkle your yeast in your warm water and allow to stand for at least 1 minute. Stir to dissolve.

2. Then mix in your remaining ingredients and stir thoroughly until your mixture forms a dough.

3. Turn your dough onto a lightly floured surface and knead for the next 5 minutes. After this time place into a bowl and allow to sit in a warm place until double in size.

4. Next preheat your oven to 475 degrees.

5. While your oven is heating up stretch your dough onto a generously greased pizza pan.

6. Spread your tomato sauce over the top of your dough and sprinkle your remaining ingredients over the top generously.

7. Place into your oven to bake for the next 10 to 15 minutes or until the bottom of your curst is a deep brown in color.

8. Remove and allow to cool slightly before serving. Enjoy.

Recipe II: Classic Pizza al Forno

This delicious pizza is one of my personal favorite dishes and once you get a taste of it yourself, it will soon become yours too.

Yield: 1 Pizza

Cooking Time: 20 Minutes

List of Ingredients:

- ½ Cup of Alfredo Sauce, Your Favorite Kind
- ½ Cup of Cheese, Ricotta Variety
- 1 Pizza Crust, Prebaked Variety
- 2 Tomatoes, Plum Variety and Sliced Thinly
- 4 Ounces of Mozzarella Cheese, Finely Shredded

AAAAAAAAAAAAAAAAAAAAAAAAAAAAAAAAAAAAAAAAAAAAAAAAA

Instructions:

1. The first thing that you will want to do is preheat your oven to 425 degrees.

2. While your oven is heating up combine both your sauce and ricotta cheese together in a medium sized bowl.

3. Next place your prebaked pizza crust onto an ungreased pizza pan.

4. Pour your ricotta mixture on top of your crust and then top off with your cheese and plum tomatoes.

5. Place into your oven to bake for the next 15 minutes.

6. Remove from oven and garnish however you like.

Recipe 12: Classic Gold and White Pizza

This is a great pizza recipe to make for your average cheese pizza lover. It is incredibly savory and very easy to make, making it the perfect recipe to make during the weekend.

Yield: 1 Pizza

Cooking Time: 40 Minutes

List of Ingredients:

- 3 Tablespoons of Olive Oil, Extra Virgin Variety and Evenly Divided
- 1 Onion, Sweet, Large in Size and Thinly Sliced
- 1 Pound of Pizza Dough, Premade
- 1 Clove of Garlic, Minced
- 4 Ounces of Cream Cheese, Soft
- ¾ Cup of Mozzarella Cheese, Finely Shredded
- ½ Cup of Romano Cheese, Finely Shredded
- ½ teaspoons of Red Pepper Flakes, Crushed

AAAAAAAAAAAAAAAAAAAAAAAAAAAAAAAAAAAAAAAAAAAAAAAAAA

Instructions:

1. The first thing that you will want to do is preheat your oven to 425 degrees.

2. While your oven is heating up, heat up your olive oil in a large sized skillet placed over medium heat. Once the oil is hot enough add in your onions and cook for the next 15 to 20 minutes or until golden in color. Make sure that you stir constantly.

3. Next place your premade pizza dough onto a lightly floured surface.

4. Then mix together your garlic and olive oil. Spread evenly on your dough.

5. Top with your cream cheese, cook onions and red pepper.

6. Top with your remaining cheese.

7. Place into your oven to bake for the next 10 to 15 minutes or until your pizza crust is light brown in color. Remove and serve right away.

Recipe 13: Lazy Cheeseburger and Sausage Pizza

This is a perfect pizza recipe to make for those who don't want to spend too much time cooking in the kitchen. This dish is not only incredibly easy to make, but it is absolutely delicious as well.

Yield: 1 Pizza

Cooking Time: 25 Minutes

List of Ingredients:

- 1 Pound of Sausage, Finely Crumbled
- 1 Pizza Crust, Fully Prepared
- ½ Cup of Mustard, Yellow Variety
- 2 Cups of Mozzarella Cheese, Finely Shredded
- ½ Cup of Onions, Finely Chopped
- 15 Dill Pickles, cut into Thin Sliced
- ¾ Cup of Cheese, Cheddar Variety and Finely Shredded

AAAAAAAAAAAAAAAAAAAAAAAAAAAAAAAAAAAAAAAAAAAAAAAAAAAA

Instructions:

1. The first thing that you will want to do is preheat your oven to 425 degrees.

2. While your oven is heating up cook up your sausage in a medium sized skillet placed over medium heat. Cook until thoroughly brown in color. Once brown in color remove and drain on some paper towels.

3. Then place your premade pizza dough onto a greased baking sheet.

4. Spread your mustard over your pizza dough and top off with your cooked sausage.

5. Spread your remaining ingredients over your dough generously, spreading your cheese over the top last.

6. Place into your oven to bake for the next 12 minutes or until your cheese begins to bubble.

7. Remove and serve while still piping hot.

Recipe 14: Personal Pan Mushroom Pizza

If you don't want to make a huge pizza but instead want to make a small one just for you to enjoy, then this is the perfect recipe for you. It makes the perfect sized pizza to be enjoyed by one person.

Yield: 1 Pizza

Cooking Time: 25 Minutes

List of Ingredients:

- 1 Mushroom, Portobello Variety and with Stem Removed
- 1 tablespoon of Spaghetti Sauce, Your Favorite Kind
- ½ Cup of Mozzarella Cheese, Finely Shredded
- ½ Tablespoons of Black Olives, Finely Sliced
- 4 Slices of Sausage, Pepperoni Variety
- 1 Clove of Garlic, Finely Chopped

AAAAAAAAAAAAAAAAAAAAAAAAAAAAAAAAAAAAAAAAAAAAAA

Instructions:

1. The first thing that you will want to do is preheat your oven to 375 degrees.

2. While your oven is heating up place your Portobello mushroom onto a generous greased baking sheet.

3. Place into your oven to bake for the next 5 minutes.

4. After this time remove and top with your remaining ingredients.

5. Place back into your oven and continue to bake for another 20 minutes or until your cheese is fully melted. Remove and enjoy immediately.

Recipe 15: Garlic Style Chicken Pizza

If you are looking for a hearty and more filling pizza dish, then this is the perfect dish for you to make. It is extremely delicious and makes for the perfect late night meal.

Yield: 1 Pizza

Cooking Time: 30 Minutes

Ingredients for Your Pizza Dough:

- 1 1/8 Cups of Water, Warm
- 1 ¼ teaspoons of Salt, For Taste
- 1 ½ teaspoons of Oil, Vegetable Variety
- 3 Cups of Flour, Bread Variety
- 2 Tablespoons of Milk, Dried and Powdered
- 2 teaspoons of Yeast, Dry and Active

Ingredients for Your Pizza:

- 2 Tablespoons of Cornmeal
- 1 Cup of Garlic, Fully Roasted
- 1 Cup of Parmesan Cheese Sauce
- ¼ teaspoons of Garlic, Fully Granulated
- 10 Ounces of Mozzarella, Finely Shredded
- 2 Chicken Breasts, Skinless, Boneless, Grilled and Fully Chopped
- ¼ of an Onion, Red in Color and Finely Diced
- 1 Tomato, Fresh and Cut into Small Wedges
- 1 Green Bell Pepper, Seeded and Finely Diced

AAAAAAAAAAAAAAAAAAAAAAAAAAAAAAAAAAAAAAAAAAAAAAAA

Instructions:

1. First place all of your ingredients for your pizza dough into a bread machine and allow to blend until a thick dough forms.

2. Next preheat your oven to 475 degrees.

3. While your oven is heating up, sprinkle a pizza pan with your cornmeal and roll onto your pizza pan.

4. Spread your sauce on top of your dough and sprinkle generously with your garlic.

5. Add a layer or cheese and top off with more garlic and your remaining pizza ingredients. Top off with more cheese.

6. Place into your oven to bake for the next 20 to 25 minutes or until your dough is light brown in color and your cheese is bubbly.

7. Remove and serve right away.

Recipe 16: Tasty Tomato and Spinach Pizza

Here is yet another healthy and delicious pizza recipe that even the pickiest of eaters are going to enjoy.

Yield: 1 Pizza

Cooking Time: 35 Minutes

Ingredients for Your Dough:

- 1 ¼ Cups of Water, Warm
- 2 Tablespoons of Olive Oil, Extra Virgin Variety
- ¾ teaspoons of Salt, For Taste
- 4 Cups of Flour, All Purpose Variety
- 1 tablespoon of Yeast, Active and Dry Variety

Ingredients for Your Toppings:

- 1 tablespoon of Olive Oil, Extra Virgin
- 3 Tablespoons of Parmesan Cheese, Finely Grated
- 1 tablespoon of Italian Seasoning, Fresh
- ¾ teaspoons of Salt, Garlic Variety
- 1 Pack of Spinach, Frozen, Thawed and Roughly Chopped
- 3 Tomatoes, Plum Variety and Sliced Thinly
- 2 Cups of Mozzarella Cheese, Skim Variety and Finely Shredded

AAAAAAAAAAAAAAAAAAAAAAAAAAAAAAAAAAAAAAAAAAAAAAAA

Instructions:

1. Using a bread machine combine all of your ingredients needed for your dough and allow to mix until you have a thick dough on your hands.

2. Once your dough is ready, turn it onto a lightly floured surface and knead for at least 10 minutes. Then roll out into a large sized circle.

3. Transfer to a large sized pizza pan that has been generously greased with some cooking spray.

4. Brush the top of your dough with some oil and season with your next 3 ingredients. Prick the dough with a fork.

5. Top off with your remaining ingredients.

6. Place into your oven to bake at 375 degrees for the next 20 to 25 minutes or until your crust is golden in color and your cheese is fully melted.

7. Then increase the heat to a broil and allow to broil for the next 5 minutes.

8. Remove and serve whenever you are ready.

Recipe 17: Spaghetti Style Pizza

If you are a huge fan of spaghetti, then this is one pizza recipe that you are going to love. It incorporates both Italian classics, making it perfect when you are craving this specific cuisine.

Yield: 1 Pizza

Cooking Time: 50 Minutes

List of Ingredients:

- 1 Pack of Spaghetti, Uncooked
- 1 Pound of Beef, Lean and Ground
- 2 ½ Cups of Spaghetti Sauce, Your Favorite Kind
- ½ Cup of Parmesan Cheese, Finely Grated
- 2 Eggs, Large in Size and Beaten
- 3 Slices of Cheese, American Variety
- 1 Pack of Mozzarella, Finely Shredded

AAAAAAAAAAAAAAAAAAAAAAAAAAAAAAAAAAAAAAAAAAAAAAAA

Instructions:

1. First preheat your oven to 350 degrees.

2. While your oven is heating up, you will want to cook your spaghetti. To do this bring a large sized pot of water to a boil over medium heat. Once the water is boiling add in your spaghetti and cook until tender to the touch. Drain and set aside for later use.

3. While your pasta is cooking, cook your ground beef in a large sized skillet placed over medium heat until brown in color. Once brown drain and crumble finely.

4. Mix your beef with your sauce.

5. Then use a large sized bowl and toss your pasta with your parmesan cheese and beaten eggs.

6. Press your pasta into a large sized pie place and top off with your sauce mixture and last with your shredded mozzarella.

7. Place into your oven to bake for the next 30 minutes.

8. Remove from oven and allow to cool slightly before serving. Enjoy.

Recipe 18: Healthy Eggplant Style Pizza

Here is yet another healthy pizza recipe that I know you are going to love. It is made with delicious eggplant which is not only incredibly healthy, but surprisingly delicious as well.

Yield: 1 Pizza

Cooking Time: 25 Minutes

List of Ingredients:

- 2 Eggs, Large in Size and Beaten
- 1 Cup of Flour, All Purpose Variety
- ½ teaspoons of Salt, For Taste
- ¼ teaspoons of Black Pepper, For Taste
- ½ teaspoons of Oregano, Dried
- 1 Eggplant, Large in Size and Sliced Finely
- ¼ Cup of Oil, Vegetable Variety
- 1 Can of Pizza Sauce, Your Favorite Kind
- 1 ½ Cups of Mozzarella, Finely Shredded

AAAAAAAAAAAAAAAAAAAAAAAAAAAAAAAAAAAAAAAAAAAAAAAA

Instructions:

1. The first thing that you will want to do is preheat your oven to 350 degrees.

2. While your oven is heating up combine your first 5 ingredients in a large sized Ziploc bag.

3. Then dip your eggplant slices into this mixture, shaking vigorously to coat.

4. Next heat up your oil in a large sized skillet placed over medium heat. Once the oil is hot enough add in your coated eggplant slices and cook until brown in color. Remove and drain on a plate lined with paper towels.

5. Place your eggplant slices on a baking sheet and top with your pizza slices and shredded mozzarella.

6. Place into your oven to bake for the next 5 to 10 minutes.

7. After this time remove from oven and serve whenever you are ready. Enjoy.

Recipe 19: Chicago Style Pizza

Even if you have never tried Chicago Style Pizza for yourself before, once you get a bite of this recipe you will want to make it over and over again. This is the perfect dish to make when you wish to impress your family with your pizza making skills.

Yield: 1 Pizza

Cooking Time: 45 Minutes

List of Ingredients:

- 1 Pound of Bread Dough, Frozen and Premade
- 1 Pound of Sausage, Italian Style
- 2 Cups of Mozzarella, Finely Shredded
- 8 Ounces of Mushrooms, Fresh and Finely Sliced
- 1 Onion, Small in Size and Finely Chopped
- 2 teaspoons of Olive Oil, Extra Virgin Variety
- 1 Can of Tomatoes, Finely Diced and Drained
- ¾ teaspoons of Oregano, Dried
- ½ teaspoons of Salt, For Taste
- ¼ teaspoons of Fennel Seed, Fresh
- ¼ teaspoons of Garlic, Powdered Variety
- ½ Cup of Parmesan, Finely Grated

AAAAAAAAAAAAAAAAAAAAAAAAAAAAAAAAAAAAAAAAAAAAAAAAA

Instructions:

1. The first thing that you will want to do is preheat your oven to 350 degrees.

2. While your oven is heating up place your dough into the bottom of a large sized baking dish and press the dough up along the sides.

3. Next place your sausage into a large sized skillet placed over medium to high heat and cook until your sausage is brown in color. Once brown in color remove the sausage and drain. Sprinkle over your dough in your baking dish.

4. Cover your sausage with some cheese.

5. Add a layer of your onions and remaining ingredients. Top off with your mozzarella and parmesan cheese.

6. Place into your oven to bake for the next 25 to 30 minutes or until your crust is golden brown in color. Remove and serve whenever you are ready.

Recipe 20: Vidalia Style Ranch Pizza

This is a great tasting pizza recipe that you can make for a large group of pizza. It is so delicious your guests will be begging you for more.

Yield: 1 Pizza

Cooking Time: 35 Minutes

List of Ingredients:

- 1 Premade Pizza Crust
- ¼ Cup of Ranch Dressing, Premade
- 2 Tablespoons of Olive Oil, Extra Virgin Variety
- 1 Vidalia, Large in Size and Sliced Thinly
- 1 teaspoon of Salt, For Taste
- 2 teaspoons of Garlic, Powdered Variety
- 1 Cup of Ranch Dressing
- 2 Tomatoes, Medium in Size and Sliced Thinly
- 1 Cup of Cheddar Cheese, Finely Shredded
- 1 Cup of Mozzarella Cheese, Finely Shredded
- ¼ Cup of Parmesan Cheese, Finely Grated
- Dash of Black Pepper, For Taste

Instructions:

1. The first thing that you will want to do is preheat your oven to 400 degrees. While your oven is heating up grease a large sized baking sheet generously.

2. Spread your premade pizza dough onto your baking sheet and spread your ranch dressing over the top. Season with your garlic powder.

3. Next heat up your olive oil in a large sized skillet and place over medium heat. Once your oil is hot enough add in your Vidalia and cook until the onion is translucent. Season with some salt and remove from heat. Top off your pizza with your cooked onion.

4. Place into your oven to bake for the next 8 to 10 minutes or until light brown in color.

5. After this time remove from your oven and top off with your remaining ingredients.

6. Place back into your oven to bake for the next 12 to 15 minutes or until your crust is golden brown in color.

7. Remove and allow to cool slightly before serving.

Recipe 21: Simple Artichoke and Garlic Pizza

This is a perfect pizza recipe to make for those who are looking to enjoy something that is not only incredibly filling, but that is also healthy as well.

Yield: 1 Pizza

Cooking Time: 30 Minutes

List of Ingredients:

- 1 Pizza Crust, Unbaked Variety
- ¾ Cup of Spaghetti Sauce, Your Favorite Kind
- 1 Jar of Artichoke Hearts, Drained and Marinated
- 1 Tomato, Medium in Size and Cut into Halves
- 2 Cloves of Garlic, Minced
- 1 Pound of Cheese, Colby and Monterey Jack Variety

AAAAAAAAAAAAAAAAAAAAAAAAAAAAAAAAAAAAAAAAAAAAAAAA

Instructions:

1. The first thing that you will want to do is preheat your oven to 450 degrees.

2. While your oven is preheating, prepare your pizza crust according to the directions on the package. Once full prepared place it onto a greased pizza pan.

3. Next pour your liquid from your artichoke hearts into a small sized skillet and bring it to a boil over medium heat. Boil for 1 minute.

4. Then add in your garlic and cook for 30 seconds.

5. Add in your artichokes and cook for at least 30 seconds. Remove from heat.

6. Next pour your sauce over your dough and sprinkle your cooked artichoke mixture over your sauce.

7. Add your tomato slices and top off with your cheese.

8. Place into your oven to bake for the next 20 minutes. Remove and serve whenever you are ready.

Recipe 22: Crab Smothered Pizza

This is a great pizza dish to make for any seafood lover out there. It is rich in taste and very filling. Once you get a taste of it I know you will want to make it over and over again.

Yield: 2 Pizzas

Cooking Time: 1 Hour and 40 Minutes

Ingredients for Your Dough:

- 3 Cups of Flour, All Purpose Variety
- 1 Pack of Yeast, Active and Dry
- 1 teaspoon of Sugar, White
- ½ teaspoons of Salt, For Taste
- 1 Cup of Water, Warm
- 2 Tablespoons of Olive Oil, Extra Virgin Variety

Ingredients for Your Toppings:

- 2 Packs of Cream Cheese, Soft
- 2 Cans of Crabmeat, Drained and Flaked
- ¼ Cup of Milk, Whole
- 1 Cup of Feta Cheese, Crumbled
- 1 teaspoon of Basil, Dried
- 1 teaspoon of Oregano, Dried
- ½ teaspoons of Garlic, Powdered Variety
- 1 Cup of Swiss Cheese, Evenly Divided

Instructions:

1. Use a large sized mixing bowl and combine all of your ingredients for your dough until thoroughly combined. Continue to stir until your mixture forms a soft dough.

2. Then turn your dough onto a lightly floured surface and knead thoroughly for the next 10 minutes.

3. Place your dough into a bowl and cover with plastic wrap. Allow to rise for the next hour.

4. After this time punch your dough down and divide it into half. Place onto a lightly floured surface.

5. Roll each dough ball into a medium sized ball and transfer to lightly greased pizza pans. Prick both pizza crusts with a fork.

6. Place into your oven to bake for the next 10 to 12 minutes or until light brown in color.

7. While your crusts are baking combine your topping ingredients together in a large sized bowl and sprinkle generous over both of your baked pizza crusts.

8. Place back into your oven to bake for the next 10 to 12 minutes or until your crust is golden brown in color and your cheese is fully melted.

9. Remove and allow to cool slightly before serving.

Recipe 23: Mexican Style Pizza

This is a great tasting pizza recipe that you are going to want to make over and over again. This dish is a little more filling than your average pizza recipe and has a bit of a kick to it.

Yield: 1 Pizza

Cooking Time: 50 Minutes

List of Ingredients:

- 1 Can of Beans, Refried Variety
- 1 Pound of Beef, Ground and Lean
- 1 Pack of Taco Seasoning, Your Favorite Kind
- 1 tablespoon of Oil, Vegetable Variety
- 4 Tortillas, Corn Variety
- 8 Ounces of Cheese, Cheddar Variety and Finely Shredded
- 8 Tablespoons of Sour Cream
- 2 Tomatoes, Roma Variety and Finely Chopped
- 2 Onions, Green in Color and Finely Chopped
- 1 Can of Green Chiles, Drained and Finely Diced
- ½ of an Avocado, Finely Diced
- 1 tablespoon of Black Olives, Finely Sliced

AAA

Instructions:

1. First heat up your refried beans in a small sized saucepan placed over low heat.

2. Then use a large sized skillet and place it over medium heat. Once it is hot enough add in your beef and cook until brown in color. Once brown add in your taco seasoning and stir well to combine. Remove from heat and set aside

3. Next preheat your oven to 350 degrees.

4. Then place a small amount of oil into a separate large sized skillet. Once the oil is hot enough add 1 tortilla to your skillet. Heat for 15 seconds and then flip. Fry for another 15 seconds. Repeat with all of your tortillas and set aside to drain on a plate lined with paper towels.

5. Spread a very thin layer of your bean onto your tortillas, followed by a thin layer of your seasoned beef and shredded cheese.

6. Then bake your tortillas in your oven for the next 20 to 30 minutes.

7. After this time slice your tortillas into wedges and garnish with your remaining ingredients. Serve whenever you are ready.

Recipe 24: Avocado and Asiago Pizza

If you have never had the chance to try out asiago cheese for yourself, then you need to try this pizza out for yourself. With the use of avocado, this make for a delicious pizza dish that you won't be able to get enough of.

Yield: 1 Pizza

Cooking Time: 25 Minutes

List of Ingredients:

- 1 Pizza Crust, Premade and Whole Wheat Variety
- 1 ½ Ounces of Prosciutto, Sliced Thinly
- 3 Ounces of Asiago Cheese, Finely Crumbled
- 2 Tablespoons of Basil, Fresh
- 2 Avocados, Peeled and Chopped
- Dash of Red Pepper Flakes, For Taste

AAAAAAAAAAAAAAAAAAAAAAAAAAAAAAAAAAAAAAAAAAAAAAAA

Instructions:

1. The first thing that you will want to do is preheat your oven to 425 degrees.

2. While your oven is heating up place your premade pizza crust onto a pizza pan.

3. Arrange your prosciutto slices over your crust evenly and top with your remaining ingredients.

4. Place your pizza in your oven to bake until your cheese is completely melted. Remove and serve whenever you are ready.

Recipe 25: Greek Style Pizza

If you are a huge fan of Greek cuisine, then I know you are going to fall in love with this recipe. It is incredibly savory and very filling. I know you are going to love it.

Yield: 4 Small Pizzas

Cooking Time: 20 Minutes

List of Ingredients:

- 4 Pita Bread, Your Favorite Kind
- 1 Cup of Ricotta Cheese, Low in Fat
- ½ teaspoons of Garlic, Powdered Variety
- 1 Pack of Spinach, Frozen, Thawed and Roughly Chopped
- 3 Tomatoes, Medium in Size and Finely Sliced
- ¾ Cup of Feta Cheese, Crumbled
- ¾ teaspoons of Basil, Dried

AAAAAAAAAAAAAAAAAAAAAAAAAAAAAAAAAAAAAAAAAAAAAAAAAA

Instructions:

1. The first thing that you will want to do is place your pita bread onto a baking sheet.

2. Then combine your ricotta cheese and garlic powder together until thoroughly combine. Spread this mixture over your pitas.

3. Top off your pizza with your remaining ingredients.

4. Place into your oven to bake for the next 12 to 15 minutes or until your pita bread is light brown in color.

About the Author

Molly Mills always knew she wanted to feed people delicious food for a living. Being the oldest child with three younger brothers, Molly learned to prepare meals at an early age to help out her busy parents. She just seemed to know what spice went with which meat and how to make sauces that would dress up the blandest of pastas. Her creativity in the kitchen was a blessing to a family where money was tight and making new meals every day was a challenge.

Molly was also a gifted athlete as well as chef and secured a Lacrosse scholarship to Syracuse University. This was a blessing to her family as she was the first to go to college and at little cost to her parents. She took full advantage of her college education and earned a business degree. When she graduated, she joined her culinary skills and business acumen into a successful catering business. She wrote her first e-book after a customer asked if she could pay for several of her recipes. This sparked the entrepreneurial spirit in Mills and she thought if one person wanted them, then why not share the recipes with the world!

Molly lives near her family's home with her husband and three children and still cooks for her family every chance she gets. She plays Lacrosse with a local team made up of her old teammates from college and there are always some tasty nibbles on the ready after each game.

Don't Miss Out!

Scan the QR-Code below and you can sign up to receive emails whenever Molly Mills publishes a new book. There's no charge and no obligation.

Sign Me Up

https://molly.gr8.com

Made in the USA
Monee, IL
21 May 2022